i

The Microexpression Master

Edited by

Rakesh Singh

Foreword   4

Table of Contents

Chapter 1:
Introduction   5

Chapter 2:
The Types Of Body Expressions   8

Chapter 3:
The Basics Of Reading Body Language   12

Chapter 4:
The Implication Of The Smallest Body Language   16

Chapter 5:
The Interpretation Of Body Languages   20

Chapter 6:
The Micro Expression Matter   25

Chapter 7:
The Benefits of Understanding the Body Expressions   27

Chapter 8:
The Skills that are Required in Understanding the Body Languages   31

Chapter 9:
Understanding What Other People are Thinking   34

Wrapping Up
The Effects of Body Language on Communication   37

Foreword

Being able to read body language is a very important skill to have in today's world. Not only will this ability help you with social ventures but also with business ones as well. Don't pass up this great information. Read ahead and learn about micro expressions.

Micro Expression Master

How To Read The Tiniest Body Language To Know What Others AreThinking

Chapter 1:

Introduction

Synopsis

Once you meet a person for the first time, you can easily tell whether you like him or not. There may be something in him or in his physical presence that distinguishes the kind of person he is. Many people say it is about intuition, instinct, or "gut feeling" but researchers discovered that there is something beyond it called micro expressions.

Micro Expressions Defined

Microexpression is defined as the brief and involuntary expression of the face shown by humans depending on the emotions experienced. Itoccurs in various high stakes solutions wherein people have something to gain or lose.

Micro expressions also occur when a particular person tries to concealall the signs of how he feels or when he is not aware of how he feels. These reactions are more difficult to hide, unlike the usual facial expressions. They are expressed in 7 universal emotions which are anger, happiness, contempt, surprise, disgust, sadness, and fear.

A person's face is the sign vehicle or medium which sends a message. When people read a facial expression, they look at separate data and draw conclusions from it. Some of this data are the muscle tone and basic structure. The wrinkles, scarring or weathering of skin may also indicate that changes definitely took place.

On the other hand, the artificial adornments like makeup, piercings, tattoos, or eyeglasses can make a personal judgment according to what a person added by his choice. But what provides more information are scowls, smiles, and frowns. These are the changes revealing obvious information regarding somebody else's immediate intentions or mood. The expression represents the intended message of a person regarding what he wants to convey.

In the following chapters, you are going to learn more about micro expression and distinguish its significance in dealing with the study of body language. Most importantly, it will help everybody to know the role of microexpression in identifying deception.

Chapter 2:

The Types Of Body Expression

Synopsis

With the help of increasing reliability and decreasing whole-body sensing technology cost, there is also an increase in understanding and increase about learning the body expressions as the dominant channel for effective communication. There are issues about the universal aspect affecting the expression, recognition and perception models or the human factors affected like culture.

Recognize The Emotions

Voices, faces, and the entire body expressions are considered as the most common emotional signals. But the emotions are expressed by the entire human body. There are several authors who investigated the recognition of the body expressions of emotions in 3 experiments. The first experiment suggested that fear as the hardest emotion to recognize. In the next experiment, the two alternatives of forced choice of facial expression categories of the compound face-body stimulus are greatly influenced by bodily expression. And for the third experiment, it is about recognition of the voice emotional tone that is influenced by the tasks irrelevant emotional expressions of the body. When taken together, it indicates the essence of the emotional body expressions in communicating along with emotional voices and facial expressions.

It is also a kind of physical and mental ability of a

non-verbal communication by human which is composed of facial expressions, eye movements, body postures and gestures. Humans interpret and send signals almost subconsciously.

There are several types of body expressions, and each of them express emotions. For the past years, more and more researches from different disciplines revealed that the body expressions are as powerful as the facial expressions in terms of conveying emotions. Here are the most common body languages seen from a person conveying different emotions or messages.

- Scrunching up the nose

- Twisting hands in the lap

- Flicking hair over the shoulder

- Scratching hair or noise

- Looking toward the ground instead of maintaining eye contact

- Placing hands on hips (to portray power)

- Getting into somebody's face (or being in

the personal space ofanother person)

Aside from these habitual body languages, eyes can express a lot also. A person may smile with his lips but not at his eyes. When a person is genuinely happy, it is reflected in their eyes. If he has a false smile,the part which surrounds the eyes does not change at all. Today, researchers added more negative and positive emotions that can be discerned.

These are:
- Relief

- Embarrassment
- Contentment
- Pride in achievement
- Amusement
- Excitement
- Guilt
- Sensory pleasure
- Shame

- Satisfaction

The physical expressions such as slouching, pointing, waving, and touching are forms of a non-verbal communication. They usually reveal various things regarding the person who is using them. One basic yet powerful signal of body language is when a person crosses his arms across his chest. It may indicate that he puts up an unconscious wall between himself and other people around. However, it may also emphasize that his arms are cold which can be clarified by huddling or rubbing his arms. In a confrontational or serious situation, it would mean that the person also expresses opposition. It can be supported when the person leaned away from the speaker.

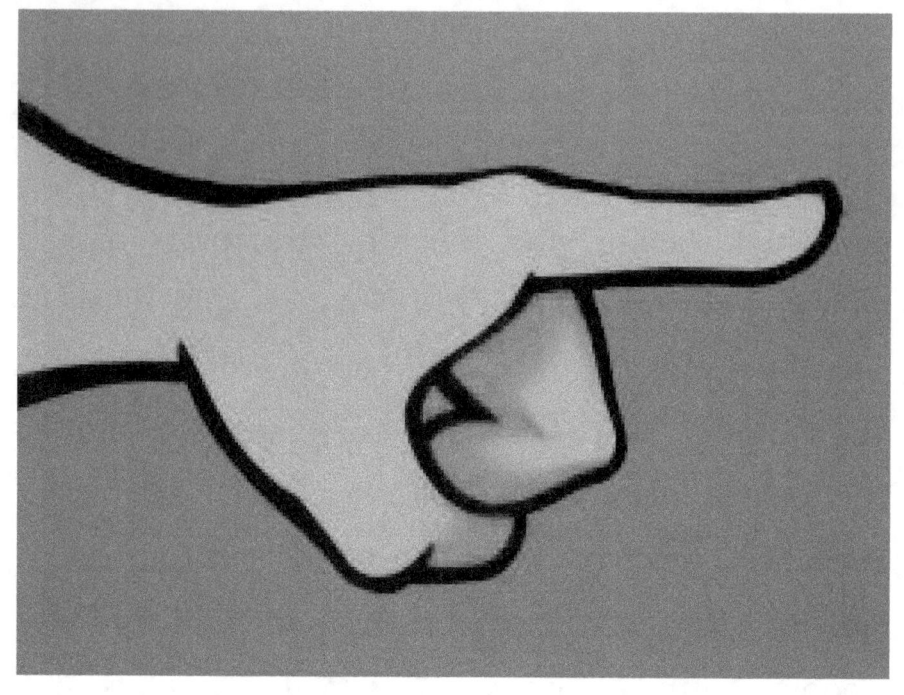

Chapter 3:
The Basics Of Reading The Body Language
Synopsis

After learning about the body language and its types, the next step is to understand the basics of reading the body language. Body language is considered a significant aspect of a modern relationship and communication. It is relevant to leadership and management and to all business and work aspects wherein communications may be physically seen and observed among individuals.

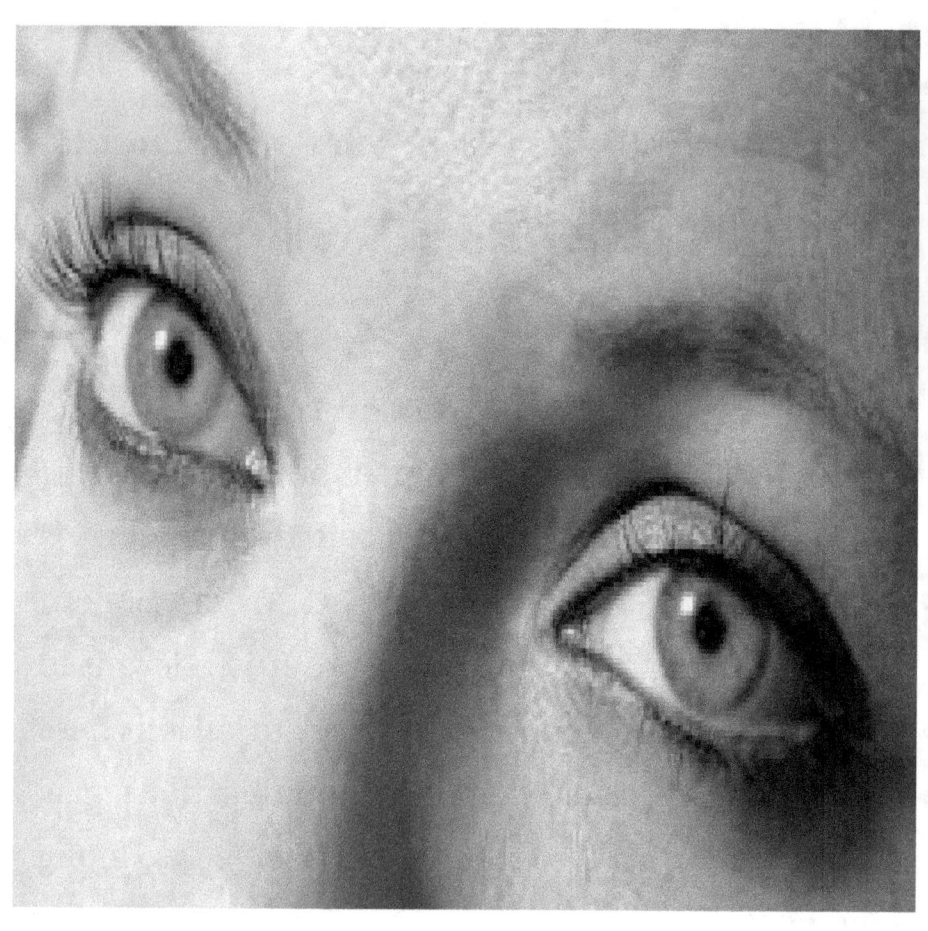

Basic Understanding

Every little expression you make emphasizes an emotion even though you may deny saying them, it will not entirely hide what you really feel inside. From flipping your hair or putting your hands on the hips, you will always find contrasting emotions in it.

Handshake

Handshaking says much more than a 'hello, nice meeting you.' Apalm-to-palm contact is said to be the most significant part of a handshake. Palm-to-palm contact is expressing an honest intention and openness; your interaction is non-threatening and sincere.

Synchrony

This body language is the signal that two people

are on the same page. Whenever a person sees that somebody else is copying his body movements or vice versa, it is a clue that they might be sharing the same mind set at that moment.

Eye contact

The rules on eye contact vary from one culture to another. Eyes are known as the most powerful of the body expression cues. They also express everything: from annoyance, to pain and happiness, and even to sexual interest. To greater or lesser extent, people 'read' others' eyes without knowing why and how. Eyes provide numerous signals and each of them tells something with regards to what they see and feel around them.

A direct contact on the eye is commonly regarded as the sign of thoughtfulness. But practiced liars are aware of this and may fake this signal. Widening the eyes indicates interest in someone or something and generally invites a positive response. Rolling of the eyes upward signals exasperation or frustration which emphasizes looking to heavens for help.

Playing with the hair

If a girl cups her hand or tucks her hair behind her ear, it may express flirting which means interest and openness.

Shoulder shrug

Shoulder shrug is one of the universal gestures used to indicate that the person does not understand or know what is been said or talked about. It is usually multiple gestures comprised of three parts: hunched shoulders, raised brow and exposed palms.

Thumb-up gesture

In some countries, this gesture has 3 meanings. It is typically used by the hitch-hikers who thumb a lift or an OK signal. When the thumb is sharply jerked upward, it is an insult signal which means 'sit on this' or 'up yours'. However, in certain countries, it means 'get stuffed.'

Body Language to Your Advantage

People who wish to manage their own body language better think about each aspect of their day and how they behave. The behavior during an everyday routine profoundly affects how the expressions are improved and shown. On the other side, you can use others' body language to your advantage. Trusting your gut is the most important thing to consider.

The body language is a way to measure the sincerity of a person about what he is saying. However, you have to ensure you are taking the proper judgment based on what you see from another person. Even though, you try to manage or understand better body language, always consider the value of their words.

Chapter 4:

The Forms And Implication Of Tiniest Body Language

Synopsis

Reading the body language gives a person an insight into whether or not somebody is sincere in his words. Most people are receiving and sending non-verbal signals without being aware of it. These are the signals that indicate what they truly feel. Every gesture or movement is a valuable key to the understanding a person's emotions at that moment. People can interpret what others are feeling or thinkingdepending on the situation.

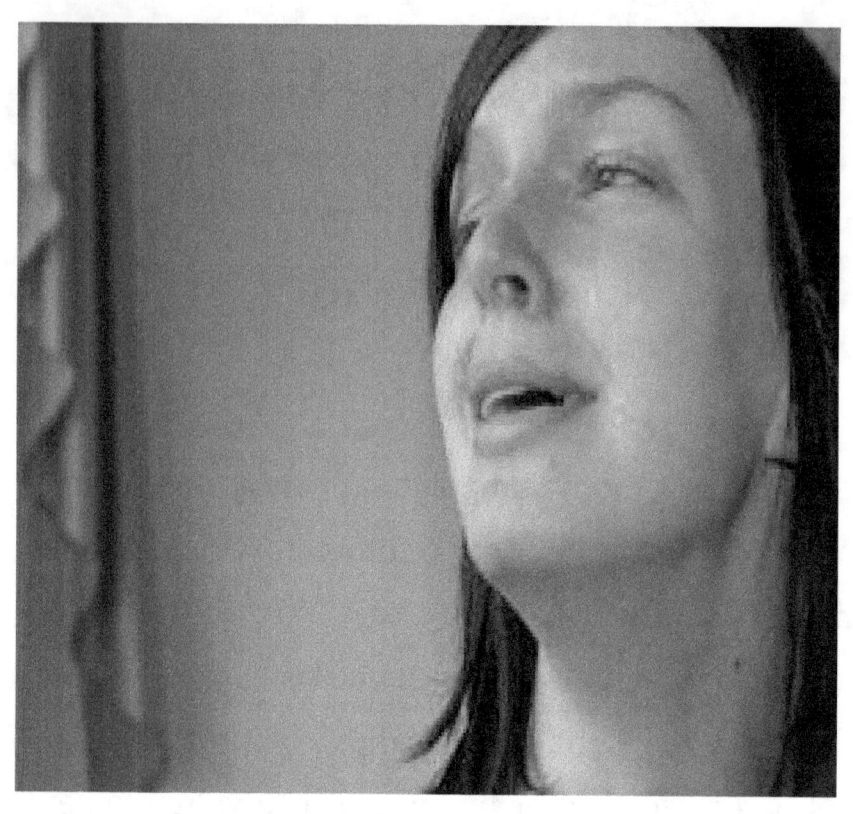

Examples Of Body Language And Their Implications

Every day, people do encounter different forms of gestures, or body language. Several signs are not the immediate signals of implications or feeling of a person. There are also traditional signs for each implication. But when noticed, they must not be taken as definite signs. Some of them are the following:

• Lying – putting a hand over the mouth; shifting in the seat; pulling the ears; touching the face. It also involves wiping the hands on the trousers to prevent sweat or fidgeting with hands.
• Stress – wetting lips frequently; shaking of legs
• Rejection – leaning back; folded or crossed arms. You may also consider multiple related gestures since folding of arms could also mean

that a person feels cold, rather than rejecting the ideas discussed.

- Defiance – hands on hips; frowning
- Aggression – stiffening of the posture, tensing of the muscles; clenched fists or leaning forward; squaring of shoulders.
- Truth – showing open hands
- Anxiety – hunched shoulders, messaging temples, different than the normal rate of breathing, nervous movements of heads.

Interpersonal Body Language

Understanding the body language is very important depending on the purpose. If you wish to approach an attractive woman, you must practice the right gestures that will help you express what you ought to say. Most men lack in the area of deciphering the implied meaning of their own actions. If you are really interested in a person, you have to primarily consider observing the way he carries himself. His movements or ways of conversation with otherpeople have something to do with his personal perception andattitude.

Knowing your own everyday body language is also essential. Smiling, eye contact and eyebrows should be included in the list of things to consider when you want to interact with another person. You also have to maintain symmetry all the time. If one area of the body is not equal with the other, it may suggest half interest in the other person. It also implies being distracted with somebody or something else. The best thing to do is to stay natural which means that you won't be thinking about the list.

The body language of the other person may be playing with hair, licking lips, maintaining eye contact, or looking at somebody 'from below' (these are the people who are trying to exaggerate the difference of height between you) and touching other's upper arm.

A person instinctively raises his eyebrows whenever he meets attractive people. Eyes have tiny glands at the bottom of the eyelids which secrete liquids like lubrication and tears. When a particular person is excited or interested, these glands secrete liquid and they give the eyes a shiny appearance.

A good posture certainly improves the confidence and the impression made by an individual. Stand and sit straight, keep your chest up and shoulders back. Once you resist reaction to your humorous remarks, other people may react more.

Dancing: A Seduction Tool

Many people perform dancing, but they do this to improve their body, as a hobby, or even as a career. But some people use it as a form of seduction. Some guys would just prefer standing somewhere and try to look cool once the alternative dances badly. For women, they treat dancing as 'safe sex' (fun and sensual activity without the downsides or risks of real sex). The ability of the guy to a close-contact dance may be viewed as the indicator of a sexual ability.

Chapter 5:

The Interpretation Of The Body Languages

Synopsis

Improving your ability to read another person's body language helps increase the emotional intelligence of a person. In most cases, it is greatly helpful in relationships. You can get along better if you have the right part of your relationship. On the other hand, basic understanding of the body expression adds to good communication skills in any circumstances.

Overview

If you are just new in learning the tiniest body language, you have to pay attention to some body parts. These body areas indicate an obvious expression of the person's emotions.

These are the following:

• Face (eye movements, mouth, eyebrows and expression) - unlike other muscles, facial muscles are connected to skin and/or other muscles.

• Head – turning away, lifting, dropping, nodding, tilting, and shaking.

• Shoulders – pulling backwards, dropping, tightening, hunching

• Legs – sitting with the legs together (crossed or wide), restless (do they shift at some points during the conversation?

• Torso – leaning backward or forward, rocking, bent, upright, angle away/towards from others, shifting in seat.

•   Hands – gestures, handshakes, and fiddling

Interpreting Body Language

All of the knowledge required to interpret the body language is safely stored in the unconscious mind of people. Some of them will be 'downloaded' from their DNA but they might lose touch with some parts of it. For every body part, there is a corresponding area which shows emotions. The language of the face goes along with the words being said and expression shown.

Mouth (Lips)

Moist and soft lips with slightly opened mouth and relaxed jaw are signs of sexual interest. Biting and licking lips suggest that someone is 'sexually provocative' according to some body language specialists. Tight lips may indicate disapproval. Biting and pulling the lips show that somebody tries to hide something as if they try to prevent a revelation of information.

Mouth (Smiling)

Faking a smile is usually hard to do. The genuine smile turns the corners of the mouth up while the eyes show a natural look.

Face (Blushing)

There are several individuals who blush easily even at minor embarrassments. Blushing may also indicate guilt. If a person does not blush immediately, there can be flushing of his face. He may feel he was caught out.

Interpreting Other Signs of Body Language

Swaying of hips

In ancient times, swaying of hips is the sign used by women to attract a partner for procreation. Men, and even some women, notice hips for that reason.

Folding of arms

It may be considered as the defensive sign either protective or angry. It can be threatening also. If somebody had puffed up his chest and had folded his arms, you might feel uncomfortable. Folding your arms can be done even when standing or sitting comfortably. However, you still have to be aware that somebody might have a different interpretation of this action.

Handshaking

A palm which is turned up slightly is inviting which is used by people when welcoming someone or starting a meeting. Close hands are more of confirming and grounding which is great for deals.

Swaggering

It may be interpreted as a sign of arrogance, and intoxication of course. It is also the macho sign just sitting with the legs apart.

The interpretation of the body language is effective when it is practiced all the time. It also involves ensuring that you are not distracted and relaxed. If you are self-obsessed or self-conscious, you will unlikely be perceptive enough.

Chapter 6:

The Micro Expression Master

Synopsis

To be a micro expression master, you have to complete the necessary things in learning the body language. There are various micro expression training sessions conducted in some part of the world to start mastering the art of body language.

Micro expressions are telling you that the emotions are concealed. However, they will never tell why or how it has been concealed. They can be the outcome of a deliberate and conscious choice wherein a person is aware of what he or she feels but prevents somebody from knowing it.

Micro Expressions Tools

METT or Micro Expression Training Tool is used to detect lies better, to make a person relaxed, be liked by other people and become more successful in their sales. But despite the efforts made to hide the signs of emotions felt, there can still be leakages in some hard-to-recognize fragments of expressions. These little challenges may happen when the emotion is just starting before an individual knows that they will act emotionally. METT is presented to train people in seeing these remarkable signals.

Facial Action Coding System or FACS is the research tool which is helpful for gauging facial expressions made by human beings. It is a system which is based anatomically for describing the observable facial movements. Every observable component of a facial movement is called an AU or action unit. All of the facial expressions may be dissected into their constituent action units.

METT also covers recognition of the concealed emotions by two types of training. The first training is in slow motion. It contrasts and compares the emotions often confused by one another. These emotions are surprise and fear; sadness and fear; disgust and anger. It includes commentary regarding how they differ from each other. This is beneficial for the people withautism and Asperger's.

The Subtle Expression Training Tool, or SETT, teaches the recognition of micro or very small signs of emotions. These are the tiniest expressions that register in a certain part of your face when an expression is obvious in the face but definitely very small. The subtle expressions may happen for various reasons. One reason is that the emotions experienced can only be very light. These expressions also occur when a certain emotion just begins and get larger if the emotions are strong.

Mini expressions happen when the strong emotions are experienced but are suppressed actively. The only leak out is the fragment of full expression. SETT training tool is developed to increase the ability of people to detect even the tiniest signals.

When you learn more about these tools, there is a greater chance of becoming a great micro expression master. Micro expressions are the fleeting expressions of the face which occur when other people are trying to suppress or repress their emotions. If they fail to do it completely, the emotion will definitely flash to their face rapidly. But 85 percent of the people have the chance to enhance their micro expressions recognition abilities through training and the tools mentioned.

The micro expression masters make use of the tiniest body language as a hint that something can be amiss. Then they are going to look for further information before they call somebody a liar.

Chapter 7:

The Benefits Of Understanding The Body Expressions

Synopsis

Learning body language is not just about detecting if a person lies to you. But rather, it has many advantages once you are able to use them properly. Aside from that, it is fun and interesting to learn since it can be easily applied to you and other people. Thus, knowing what the benefits of understanding the body expression are is also important.

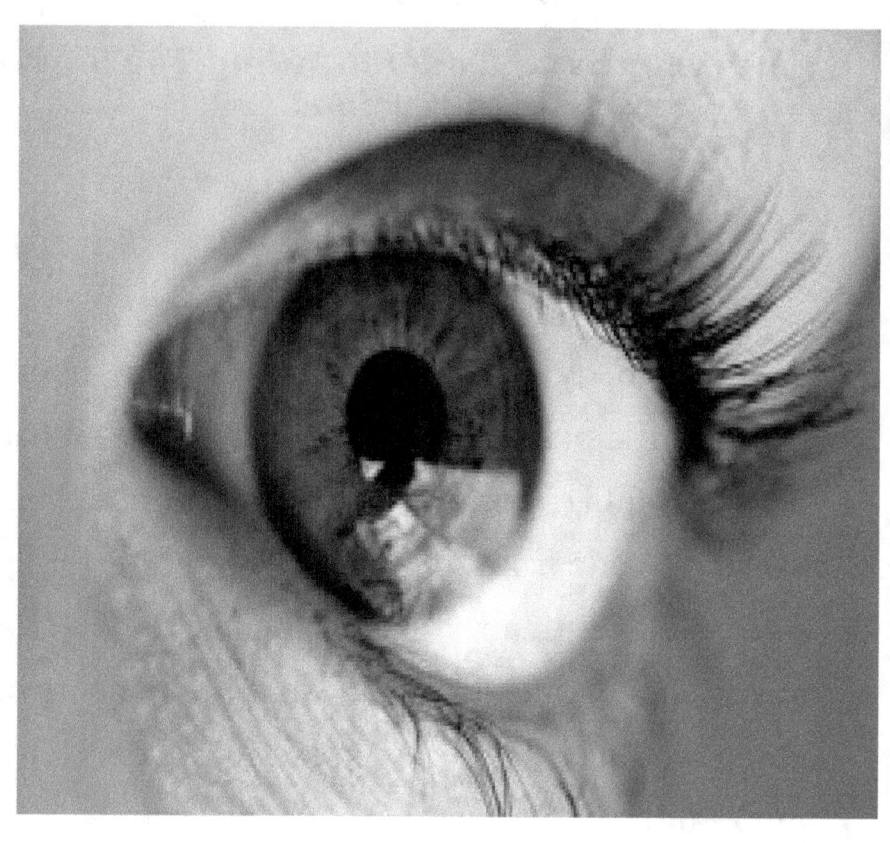

The Essence Of Body Language

People can never live without one another since they are social beings. Communication takes place once they are in contact with other individuals. This communication indicates something about the kind of relationship among people. They make use of written and spoken language and both communicate the thought and emotion of a person.

Subconscious Expression

Most of the time, the body language happens unconsciously. But the body impact the quality of communication. Take note that the body language reveals various meanings among cultures. The way people interpret the body expressions depends on specific situation including the relationship between people. Body language is interlinked with the whole pattern of behavior and spoken language from certain individuals.

Expression Of Feelings

Body language can be an effective way to express feelings and emotions toward something or somebody. People can show their real feelings by becoming aware of the body language. Research shows that body language plays a huge role in the first impression someone makes.

To make a good impression, it is essential that a person is knowledgeable enough and has the ability to control his body language. It plays a vital role in the intuition since it provides messages about other people that can be interpreted at the intuitive level.

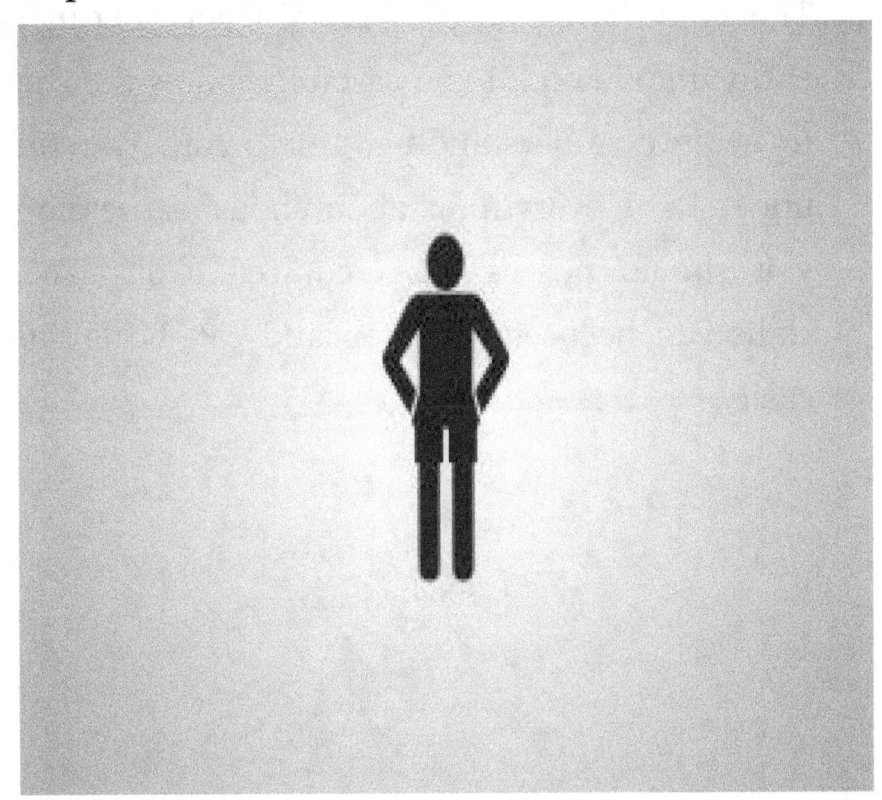

Chapter 8:

The Skills that Are Required In Understanding BodyLanguages

Synopsis

The body language of a certain person can be easily understood if you carefully follow the steps to achieve understanding. But before you fully understand everything about body expressions, you should possess the required skills. These skills can be useful to you and can be learned easily.

Basic Skills Needed to Understand Body Expressions

Every person has his own strategies in understanding what other people feel or say. But it is very important that you have the skills to successfully achieve what you intend to know. Here are some of the essential skills needed to understand body language:

Social Skills

Social skills are useful when observing the signals that other people are sending out through their body language. Some individuals can read them naturally but some are notoriously oblivious. The good news is that even with little attentiveness, you are going to learn to read the body language and with enough time to practice, it will be second nature.

Good Communication Skills

Good communication skills should be present in those who want to become micro expression masters. It will be applied whenever you are trying to observe different emotions and their implications. It is also the skill which will develop your confidence.

Eye Contact

Eye contact is considered as an essential aspect of dealing with other people most especially when you just meet for the first time. Having good eye contact indicates interest and respect in what the other person says. People should maintain eye contact for 60 to 70 percent of time. However, it is also important to be aware about the cultural differences, so you have to be careful.

Hand Gestures

The way you sway your hands indicates something so you have to learn to use different hand gestures depending on the emotions and feelings you want to express. The gestures of palm down are generally aggressive and dominant, most especially when there are no movements or bending between the forearm and wrist.

A slight change in your body expression may have an amazing impact on people surrounding you. There are helpful sources that give practical tips on how to understand and use body language.

Chapter 9:

Understanding What Other People Are Thinking

Synopsis

To have good communication with other people, both of you should understand what each one is trying to express. Understanding what other people are thinking is very important for it is the only way of getting new messages from them. When you are able to understand what the other person is trying to say, you can receive new information and do the corresponding task.

There are some rules to understand other people and prevent emotional upsets, social errors, and conflicts. Knowing some of them will at least add your knowledge and awareness.

Rules in Understanding People

Rule 1: Do Not Blame Malice For What Is Explained ByConceit

You have to think that people do not actually care about you. It does not mean they are hurtful or mean but they are simply focused on themselves.

Rule 2: Some Social Behaviors Have Been Explicit

This rule states that most of the intentions in some actions are latent. If an individual feels angry or depressed, it may result in behaviors that will distort their real feelings.

Rule 3: Behavior Is Greatly Caused By Selfish Altruism

Saying that everybody is totally selfish is a gross exaggeration. It definitely ignores all the acts of sacrifice, love and kindness that keep the world from working. Most of the behavior works from the selfish altruism principles.

Rule 4: People Generally Have Poor Memories

People are known for their trouble in keeping information in their mind. Most of the time, this information is not applicable to themselves. They will remember more about your similarities thanthe differences.

These are just some of the rules that will reveal the realistic views of people. People are usually giving their best but still make some mistakes and suffer from their unintended self-absorption.

Wrapping Up

The Effects Of Body Language On Communication

Body language is an outward reflection of the emotional condition ofa person. For instance, the act of folding arms indicates that the person is trying to put up an unconscious barrier between himself and other people around him and feel more secure. But in an amicable situation, it would mean that the person thinks about what has been discussed. In a confrontational or serious situation, it means expression opposition.

The key to understanding the body language is reading the emotional condition of a person while listening to what they say. It also includes noting of circumstances related to what they say. When somebody is intuitive or perceptive about other people, it may be referred to the ability of reading other people's body expressions or comparing the cues with the verbal signs.

Being perceptive indicates that you have the ability to detect the contradiction in somebody's words and body language. The ability to understand the thoughts and attitudes of a person through their behavior is the original system of communication utilized by humans before speaking the language existed.

The body language is the product of both environmental and genetic influences. The blind children will laugh and smile even if they never saw a smile in their entire life. It is also an essential ingredient in the social differentiation. Various languages have been involved in different bodily and facial movements. Most of the genetic or inborn communication gestures or signals are the same from in countries across the globe. However, the acquired gestures may change depending on the cultural differences. For example, the act of frowning shows that you are angry while the act of smiling indicates that you are happy.

The ability of working out what is happening with a certain person can be simple but not totally easy. You may be a great reader when you consistently practice the methods incorporated in your work. Learn some helpful exercises that will surely activate your skills in reading non verbal gestures.

Body language is an important communications because it definitely dominates the work spoken. The way people communicate plays an important role in making a great first impression. It is a dominant factor which includes posture, handshake, and even the way you dress.

There is no doubt that 90 percent of the leaders throughout history across the globe are good orators. Most of the company directors also belong to this amazing fact since they provide great presentations.

They are all aided by their special abilities of communicating in public or large groups of people.

If you are trying to send out a message with professionalism, make sure that you are presentable in the way that you stand with an upright posture, open body language, good eye contact, and have a firm handshake. Your clothing should also be appropriate to a work situation and should be neat. Your voice must be produced to express your confidence.

www.ingramcontent.com/pod-product-compliance
Lightning Source LLC
Chambersburg PA
CBHW062359290526
45794CB00003B/1009